truly me™ Shine Bright

Discover your unique talents with quizzes,
activities, crafts—and more!

by Carrie Anton
illustrated by Marilena Perilli
and Flavia Conley

Published by American Girl Publishing
Copyright © 2015 American Girl

Questions or comments? Call 1-800-845-0005,
visit **americangirl.com**, or write to Customer Service,
American Girl, 8400 Fairway Place, Middleton, WI 53562-0497.

Printed in China
15 16 17 18 19 20 21 LEO 10 9 8 7 6 5 4 3 2 1

Editorial Development: Melissa Seymour, Trula Magruder
Art Direction and Design: Paula Riley, Lisa Wilber, Sigrid Hubertz
Production: Jeannette Bailey, Judith Lary, Paula Moon, Kendra Schluter, Cynthia Stiles
Photography: Radlund Photography, Youa Thao
Craft Stylist: Carrie Anton
Wardrobe Stylist: Aubre Andrus
Hair Stylist: Lynée Ruiz, Ashley Franklin
Doll Stylist: Meghan Hurley
Illustrations: Marilena Perilli, Flavia Conley

Stock Photography: page 5 (dog), © iStock.com/jenjen42; page 6 (shoe girl),
© iStock.com/DanielBendjy; page 6 (yoga girl), © iStock.com/blackwaterimages;
page 33 (cat), © iStock.com/OlgaMiltsova; page 33 (girl with note), © iStock.com/RichLegg.

Dear Reader,

Singing, acting, dancing, reciting a poem, and playing an instrument are all types of performances. If these are things you love to do, either onstage or just in front of your doll, then you have a talent! And when you have a talent, you should develop it. It doesn't matter how good you are at these things, because the more you practice your talent, the better you will become. Simply being interested in performing is the first step toward being a performer.

No matter how you want to express your creative gift, this book can help. We've packed in quizzes, activities, and crafts that will celebrate the skills you have and inspire you to be even more artistic and imaginative than you already are.

Ready? Lights, camera, roll out the fun!

Your friends at American Girl

When you see this symbol ✋, it means you need an adult to help you with all or part of the task. ALWAYS ask for help before continuing. Ask an adult to approve all craft supplies before you use them—some are not safe for kids. When creating doll crafts, remember that dyes from supplies may bleed onto your doll or her clothes and leave permanent stains. Use lighter colors when possible, and check your doll often to make sure the colors aren't transferring to her body, her vinyl, or her clothes. And never get your doll wet! Water and heat increase dye rub-off.

I believe that *every* person is born with talent.

—Maya Angelou

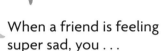

Be a Star

When it comes to stardom, how will you shine?

If you've always dreamed of seeing your name in lights but aren't quite sure what your famous future holds, this quiz is for you!

1. When a friend is feeling super sad, you . . .

a. cry right along with her.

b. create a playlist of songs that will make her smile.

c. make and send her a special card.

d. invite her to your house for a sleepover.

e. ask her to go for a bike ride.

f. draw her a silly picture.

2. The best kind of dog is one that . . .

a. does cool tricks.

b. howls really loudly.

c. cuddles with you while you write in your journal.

d. plays nicely with all the other dogs at the park.

e. runs an obstacle course with ease.

f. makes you laugh when he eats a treat.

3. Your teacher announces a class party and needs helpers. You volunteer to . . .

a. lead a game of charades.

b. bring in speakers for music.

c. decorate.

d. cut and pass out cake.

e. set up an area for the dance floor.

f. make props for funny pictures.

5. Your teacher often has to ask you to . . .

a. stop talking.

b. stop humming.

c. speak up.

d. stop passing notes.

e. sit still.

f. stop making faces.

6. When studying for a test, which of the following strategies helps you memorize facts?

a. repeatedly reciting them

b. setting the facts to a favorite tune

c. writing them down over and over again

d. flash cards

e. breaking them into steps, practicing one thing until it's perfect before moving to the next

f. thinking up silly-sounding mnemonic devices

4. Your favorite shoes . . .

a. are brightly colored and bold.

b. match your favorite outfit perfectly.

c. are super comfy.

d. look just like the ones your friends have.

e. are sporty and stylish sneakers.

f. have mismatched colored laces.

7. Your cool aunt is taking you out for a special day. You ask to go to a . . .

a. movie.

b. parade.

c. book signing.

d. theme park.

e. yoga class.

f. comic-book store.

Answers

Amazing Actress

If you answered **mostly a's,** get ready for your close-up. You have a knack for remembering lines, can cry on command, and are able to pull off a convincing performance whether it's funny, sad, or mysterious. Improve your acting chops by learning more about different people, cultures, and locations. Before you know it, you'll be landing leading roles!

truly me Turn to "Play Time" on page 32 to make your acting debut.

Master of Music

If you answered **mostly b's,** you've got the beat. Whether it's playing an instrument or belting out a high note, you've got rhythm in your soul. Sing or play your heart out best by listening to all kinds of music. Pop, classical, rock and roll, bluegrass, jazz, and more are all sources of inspiration.

truly me Turn to "Silly Songs" on page 23 for lyrics that will have you hitting highly funny notes.

7

Behind-the-Scenes Queen

If you answered **mostly c's,** you're ready to run the show. Most performances aren't possible without the creative genius of writers, directors, costume designers, and others. Even if being center stage isn't your thing, it doesn't mean you can't wow an audience. Customize your craft by keeping a creativity journal. Write down all your ideas for stories and songs, and draw pictures and make collages to bring them to life.

TV Host with the Most

If you answered **mostly d's,** your pleasant personality is perfect for cooking with master chefs, interviewing red-carpet celebrities, and playing games with audience members for cash and prizes. You're comfortable having convos with all kinds of people and can fill awkward silence with something interesting to say. Kick your hosting skills up a notch by finding opportunities to speak in front of groups.

truly
me Turn to "Costume Designer" on page 29 to add star appeal to a performance.

truly
me Turn to "Family Star Search" on page 38 to get your interviewing skills in super shape.

Steps Sister

If you answered **mostly e's,** you have some fancy feet. Spinning, tapping, leaping, and sashaying feel as familiar as walking and running. You tend to have a lot of energy but can still be quite focused and coordinated. No two left feet here! You love to spend time stretching your muscles and your mind. The more flexible you are with both, the better you'll be at catching on quickly to challenging choreography.

Funny Girl

If you answered **mostly f's,** you're a lot of laughs. Humor is your thing, and you love nothing more than to make other people smile. Jokes, gags, and impersonations are how you get the crowd chuckling. To become even funnier, learn about current events by watching the news and reading magazines. Hilarious things happen every day; you just need to be in the know.

truly
me Turn to "Dancing Dots" on page 22 for toe-tapping fun.

truly
me Turn to "Be Awesome" on page 30 for lots of ideas on how to share and spread smiles.

VIP Party

Make it a movie night starring you and your friends.

Host a party that is all about a performance featuring you and three of your friends. Celebrate the cinema through creative crafts, games, decor, and more! And don't forget to save some seats for your dolls!

Activities

Paper Gowns

Make instant glam looks for your dolls using only **tissue paper.** Set a **timer** for 10 minutes, and see how quickly each guest can put together a gown that is red-carpet ready. Ask your parents and siblings to judge the best looks.

Award Night

Turn **star-shaped balloon weights** into best-friend awards. Punch out the **star tags** in the back of this book and attach them to the weights using an **adhesive dot.** Some award ideas have been given; use the blank tags to create your own categories!

Make a Move

Choose a favorite movie—one you've seen before—for you and your girl crowd to see. Make a list of words, actions, or actors that pop up throughout the film. For each item on the list, assign a dance move, such as a twirl, jazz hands, or a jump. Whenever this happens in the movie, you and your guests have to do that move.

Charades

Hand each guest **five slips of paper** and a **pencil.** Start with a category like "movies." Ask guests to write down the title of movies they love on each slip of paper. Fold up the papers, and put them in a **bowl.** Without talking, a guest chooses a piece of paper from the bowl but doesn't show anyone what's written on it. She acts out whatever is written on the slip of paper. The girl who guesses correctly goes next.

Crafts

Play Props

Put on your own play with fun handheld **costume props**. Remove the **pop-outs** provided in the back of this book. Attach each pop-out to a **short wooden dowel** (found at craft stores) to make for easy holding. Make up some scripts with your friends, and act away!

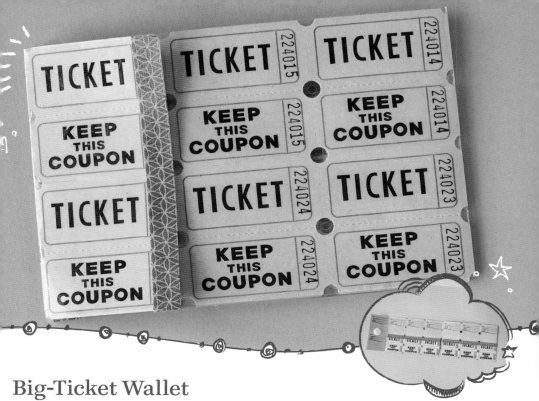

Big-Ticket Wallet

You'll need:

- A double roll of raffle tickets (available at party stores)
- Tape
- Clear packing tape
- Decorative paper tape (optional)
- Adhesive hook-and-loop closure

Instructions:

1. Tear off 2 double rows of 7 tickets and 2 double rows of 3 tickets.

2. Line up the rows of 7 tickets so that they make a rectangle 4 tickets high and 7 tickets across. Use a few small pieces of tape along the ticket backs to hold the rows together.

3. Cover each of the 3-ticket rows with clear packing tape so that both sides are covered.

4. Tape the 3-ticket pieces to the back of the large main piece to make pockets, as shown. Use clear packing tape to secure the bottom and outside edges. If needed, trim ends a bit for easy closure.

5. Decorate with paper tape, if you like.

6. Between the pockets, fold the wallet in half. Attach the adhesive hook-and-loop closure to the remaining panel and front of the wallet to close.

Favors

Star Sipper

Show a friend how much she sparkles in your life with a star-themed sipper. Fill a **plastic cup** with **star stickers, star erasers,** and other star stuff. Slip a **punch-out tag** from the back of this book onto the **straw** for the perfect party favor.

Thanks for Popping By!

Attach the **"Thanks for Popping By!" stickers** to **microwave popcorn bags** to give to friends as tasty movie-night favors.

Marquee

Turn a **trifold cardboard display** (available at craft stores) into a movie marquee. With help from an adult, cut the display in half. Attach **poster letters** (available at craft stores) to black and white **poster board** to announce the party. Decorate the board with other fun pieces, such as tickets and stars, and set it out or hang it for all to see.

Walk of Fame

Surprise your friends with a red-carpet entrance into your party. Cut in half lengthwise a **long red plastic tablecloth** (available at party stores). **Tape** the short ends together, and lay it on the floor for the perfect red carpet. Take it the next step by adding **gold stars made from poster board** with your famous friends' names.

Decor

Food

Popcorn Bar

Let guests mix their own movie-viewing munchies. Set up a snack stand with **popcorn** and shakers of seasonings such as **Parmesan cheese**, **cinnamon sugar**, and **cocoa**. Include bowls of **pretzels**, **candy**, **nuts**, and **marshmallows** that girls can add to their corn. Provide **paper bags** for your guests to fill up, shake to mix, and enjoy.

Root Beer Floats

Add scoops of **vanilla ice cream** to each guest's mug and top off with **root beer** and a **straw** for fantastic sipping.

Popcorn Cupcakes

Make a sweet movie treat with popcorn-topped cupcakes. Place **store-bought or homemade frosted cupcakes** in **red-and-white liners** and add **premade caramel popcorn** to the tops.

Dancing Dots

Design your own dance with cute cue cards.

Step to the beat using the **punch-out cards** provided in the back of the book to choreograph your own dance. Toss the Dancing Dots cards on the floor at random, or create your own unique moves.

Nod Head

Hop

Twirl

Shooting Stars

Decorate your space for the star that you are.

Let your star power shine with a garland curtain made from **punch-out stars.** Attach the stars provided in the back of the book along **three 48-inch lengths of ribbon or string** using a **glue stick** or **clear tape.** With a parent's permission, hang **two plastic removable wall hooks** about 12 to 18 inches across from each other. Knot one end of the garlands together and hang on one hook. Sweep the garlands to the side to hang on the second hook. Adjust the garlands to loop down at different lengths.

Silly Songs

These lyrics are sure to make you giggle!

Fill in the blanks—then perform your silly song for your doll and friends.

Song One

1. An action word, 2 syllables:_____

2. A size:_____

3. An object:_____

4. A girl's name:_____

5. Another action word:_____

6. A location:_____

7. A gem:_____

8. Another location:_____

9. An adjective:_____

10. Another object:_____

11. Another action word:_____

12. Another action word:

_____

13. Another object:

_____

14. A time of day:

_____

Lyrics (sung to "Twinkle, Twinkle, Little Star")

[1], [1], [2] [3],
How [4] [5] what you are.
Up above the [6] so high,
Like a [7] in the [8].
When the [9] [10] is gone,
When he nothing [11] upon,
Then you [12] your [2] [13],
[1], [1], all the [14].

Song Two

1. A size:_____

2. An object:_____

3. Another size:_____

4. Another size:_____

5. Another object:_____

6. Another object:_____

7. An action word (past tense):_____

8. Another action word:_____

9. Another action word:_____

10. Another action word:_____

Lyrics (sung to "I'm a Little Teapot")

I'm a [1] [2]
[3] and [4].
Here is my [5],
Here is my [6].
When I get all [7] up,
Hear me [8]!
Just [9] me over
and [10] me out!

Song Three

1. A girl's name:

_____

2. An animal:

_____

3. A type of material:

_____

4. A color:

_____

5. An object:

_____

6. An action word:

_____

Lyrics (sung to "Mary Had a Little Lamb")

[1] had a little [2],
Little [2], little [2].
[1] had a little [2];
Its [3] was [4] as [5].
And everywhere that [1] went,
[1] went, [1] went,
Everywhere that [1] went
The [2] was sure to [6].

And the Award Goes to . . . YOU!

Start working on your acceptance speech.

Start

Your talents have been nominated for a future award. Follow the maze to see what fate awaits you.

A TV Star Award for You

Did you come out this exit?

You're going to shine on the small screen. TV is the place for you. You could play the lead in a funny sitcom. But it's not just about acting. Be the star of your own talk show, write an awesome theme song, direct a mystery miniseries, or inform the world as a top-notch news anchor. Your hard work in any category will be rewarded!

A Movie Star Award for You

Did you come out this exit?

Work on your paparazzi smile, because your talents are going to be on the silver screen for all to see. Movies will be your ticket, whether it means you're calling the shots behind the camera, playing the lead in an action movie, or composing the music that has everyone singing. Lights, camera, and action are in your future!

A Super Singer Award for You

Did you come out this exit?

Your voice will be the star of any show. Find the type of music that's right for you, be it rock and roll, blues, pop, jazz, country, rap, or a mix that is all your own. The more unique your sound, the better you'll stand out from the rest of the artists. Go on and hit those high notes!

A Theater Star Award for You

Did you come out this exit?

The theater is where you'll feel finest. The bright lights of Broadway will be your home away from home. Star in a play. Choreograph the dances of a major musical. Belt out the notes of an operatic solo. Or be in charge of the entire production. The stage is in your hands; make it shine!

Costume Designer

Bring paper characters to life with clothing created by you!

Put on a paper-doll performance using the punch-outs provided in the back of this book. Plan your play, color in the costumes of the characters, and then attach the clothes with adhesive dots. When everyone is dressed for the stage, entertain an audience of friends and family.

Be Awesome

Use your special talent to send smiles everywhere.

Have you ever watched someone laugh and then couldn't help but laugh, too? You probably didn't even know what was so funny, yet you were still in stitches. It's the same way with smiles; they're contagious. You can make the world a happier place by using your talents to cheer up others. When you make people smile, they will be inspired to use their talents to do the same thing. The smiles will go on for miles, all thanks to what makes you unique. Need some ideas on how to get started? Here's a list!

1. Sing a song at an assisted-living center.

2. Play an instrument at a talent show.

3. Make up a dance with your friends at recess.

4. Write a script to perform with your sister.

5. Paint a picture, and send it to a faraway family member.

6. Interview your grandparents about their childhoods and record the interview to keep.

7. Use old socks to make puppets.

8. Use paper and fabric scraps to make costumes for your dolls to wear in a musical.

9. Ask to read books at your library's toddler story hour, using silly voices for all the characters.

10. Write and perform a song at your family's holiday dinner.

11. Make a gift for your friend's birthday instead of buying her something.

12. Tuck a joke into the pocket of your dad's coat.

13. Put on a water dance in the pool for your friends.

14. Make and play musical instruments using bottles, boxes, utensils, and smooth-edge cans.

15. Sing a bedtime song to your little brother.

16. Build a puppet-theater stage, and perform for the neighborhood kids.

17. Draw a picture of your family to hang on the fridge.

18. Paint funny faces on rocks for your mom to put in her garden.

19. Create a playlist perfect for each of your family members.

20. Turn paper plates and paper bags into masks.

Play Time

Take the quiz to find out which plot is perfect for your performance.

Want to star in a play that will keep your audience on the edge of their theater seats? Answer the following questions to discover which type of story should set your scene.

1. My favorite part of the circus is the . . .

a. trapeze act. It must feel like flying!

b. magician. How did he do that?

c. car of clowns. My sides hurt from laughing!

2. At my last birthday party, we . . .

a. had an enchanted-garden tea party.

b. had a scavenger hunt that my mom set up in the house.

c. went to the arcade to play all kinds of games.

3. If you could have any secret power, which one would it be?

a. the power to time-travel

b. invisibility

c. the ability to move things with my mind

4. Last night I had a dream that I was . . .

a. a mermaid swimming underwater.

b. a ghost floating through an empty building.

c. walking around in a world that was upside down.

5. What animal best describes you?

   a. a colorful macaw

   b. a black cat

   c. a silly chimpanzee

6. Where is your favorite hangout spot?

   a. my backyard treehouse

   b. a secret nook I set up in my closet

   c. in the family room with my siblings and parents

7. You've been invited to a costume party. Which outfit do you wear?

   a. the orange dragon with purple polka dots

   b. the masquerade ball gown and sparkly eye mask

   c. the silly doughnut costume covered in multicolor sprinkles

8. When the teacher disciplines me in class, it's usually for . . .

   a. daydreaming when I should be listening.

   b. passing notes secretly to a friend.

   c. making other kids laugh.

Answers

Fantasy Land

If you answered **mostly a's,** put on a play that whisks your audience away to imaginary lands you've only cooked up in your dreams. Give characters powers that don't exist in everyday life. Maybe animals can talk to people, or people can shrink or grow whenever they please. Stretch your mind, and let your creativity run free.

Scene Starter:
A frail sorceress enters the enchanted forest filled with talking trees and comes upon a . . .

Air of Mystery

If you answered **mostly b's,** put on a play that keeps your audience guessing. Grab them from the very beginning, and put on a show that doesn't let them go until a big reveal at the very end. The idea is to create a story line that makes the audience wonder what's going to happen, and only you hold the answers.

Scene Starter:
It was a strong, sweet smell coming from two doors down that first caught my attention. But when I opened the door, I never expected to find . . .

Cool Comedy

If you answered **mostly c's,** put on a play that will make your audience laugh. Jokes, silly names, funny actions, and kooky costumes are great was to get everyone rolling. Everyone loves a good giggle, and humor is sure to get a standing ovation.

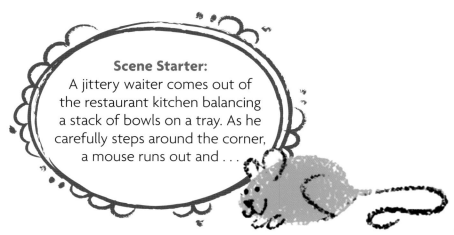

Scene Starter:
A jittery waiter comes out of the restaurant kitchen balancing a stack of bowls on a tray. As he carefully steps around the corner, a mouse runs out and . . .

Dazzling 'Dos

Shine onstage with hair accessories that are as bright as you.

You can look and feel like a glamour girl on and off the stage with barrettes, headbands, and bobby pins with a touch of bling. Wear these easy-to-make styles that are sure to be showstoppers.

Glamour Headbands: Rolls of **adhesive rhinestones** can turn plastic into something fantastic. Add **fake jewels** to make a tiara-inspired topper.

Blingy Barrettes: Add pizzazz to **plain snap barrettes** with **stick-on rhinestones** (available at craft and scrapbooking stores). Line up the gems along each side, or layer them for even more eye-catching appeal.

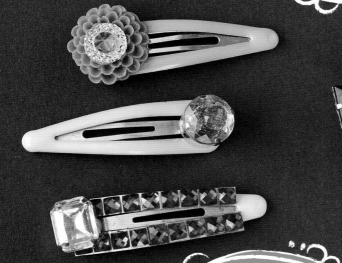

Poppin' Pins: Hold your hair back in style with a glammed-up **gem bobby pin.**

Family Star Search

Interview your family to see how each person is special.

Sometimes being a star has nothing to do with being onstage. Instead, it's how bright you shine as a person. People you know have done lots of cool things—visited distant countries, met interesting people, and overcome huge obstacles. These experiences are what make them unique—just like having a special talent. Use the questions on the next page to interview your family members. Write down or record their answers to keep in a paper or digital scrapbook.

Questions

1. What is your full name?

2. When and where were you born?

3. Do you have siblings?

4. Did you have any pets? If so, what kind and what were their names?

5. What was your childhood home like?

6. Who was your best friend and why?

7. What games did you play with your friends?

8. What was your favorite toy?

9. What was your favorite subject in school?

10. What kind of music did you like to listen to?

11. Who were your childhood heroes?

12. What is your favorite childhood memory?

13. Did you play sports or participate in other extracurricular activities in school? If so, which sport or activity?

14. What kind of clothes did you wear?

15. What is the best place you've ever visited? Why did you like it?

16. Is there a place that you one day hope to see? If so, where is it and why do you want to visit?

17. Who is the most interesting person you've ever met? What did you like about him or her?

18. What is your profession, and how did you choose it?

19. Do you ever wish you had tried a different career? If so, what?

20. What has been your proudest moment?

Here are some other American Girl books you might like:

Doll Star

Doll Art Studio

Doll Tees Felt Fashions

Doll Dining

Doll Travel

play@
☆ American Girl™

Discover online games, quizzes, activities,
and more at **americangirl.com**

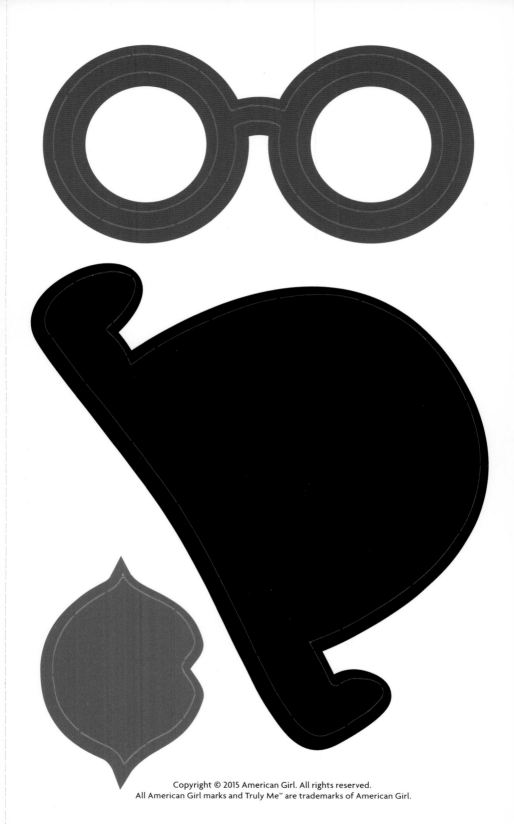

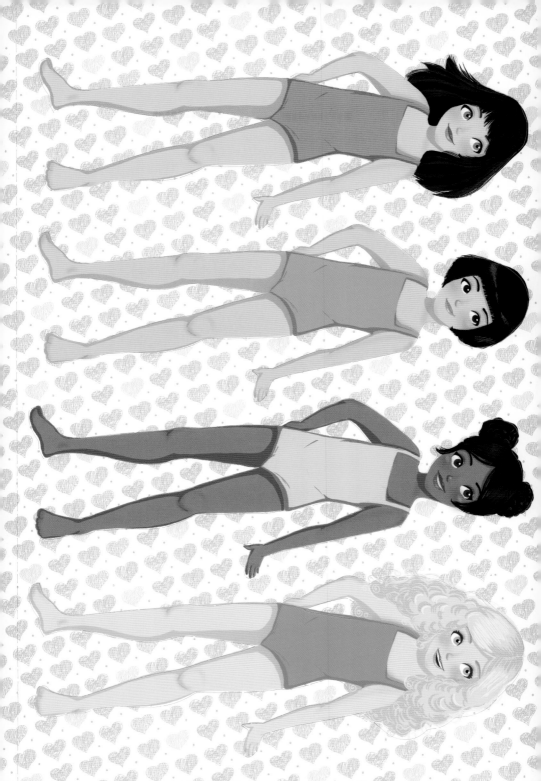

Shake Hands

Hands Up

Kick

Twirl

Hop

Touch the Floor

Twist Hips

Snap
Fingers

Step
Forward

Step
Backward

Nod
Head

Shake
Shoulders

Make Up
a Silly
Move

Run in
Place

Star Friend

Star Friend

Star Friend

Star Friend

Star Friend

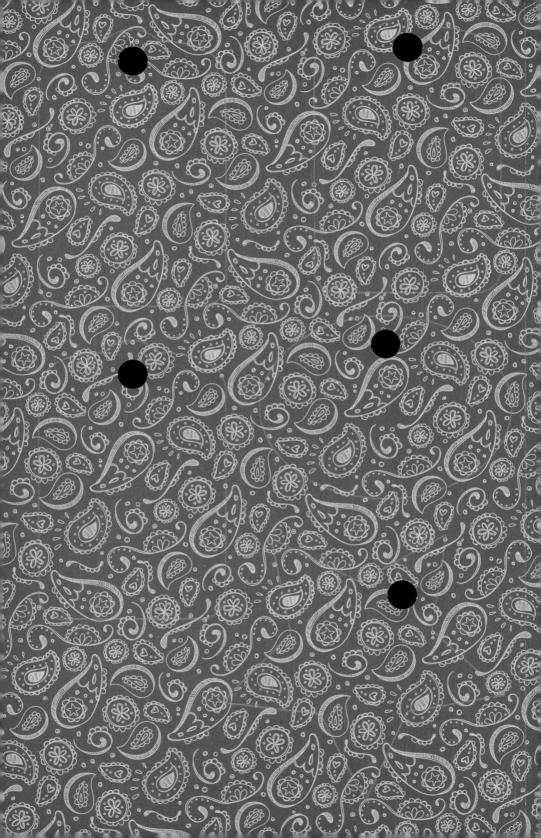

Thanks for Popping By!

Thanks for Popping By!

Thanks for Popping By!

Thanks for Popping By!

Thanks for Popping By!

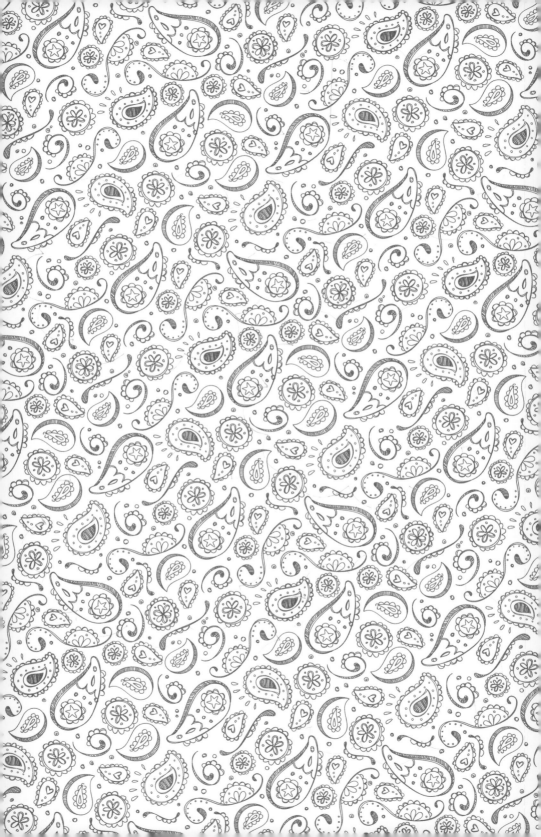

Best Smile

Best Hug

Funniest Jokes

Best Listener

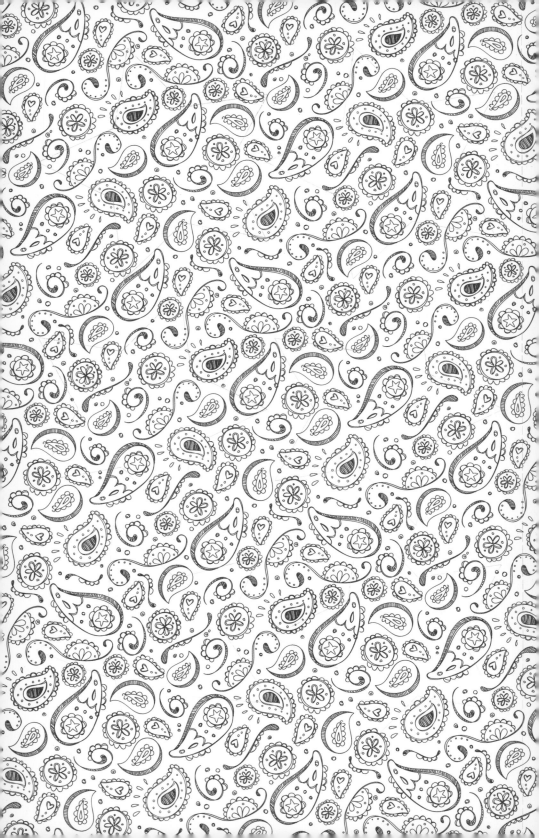

Best in
Fashion

Best
Helping
Hand

Best in
Sports

Most
Creative

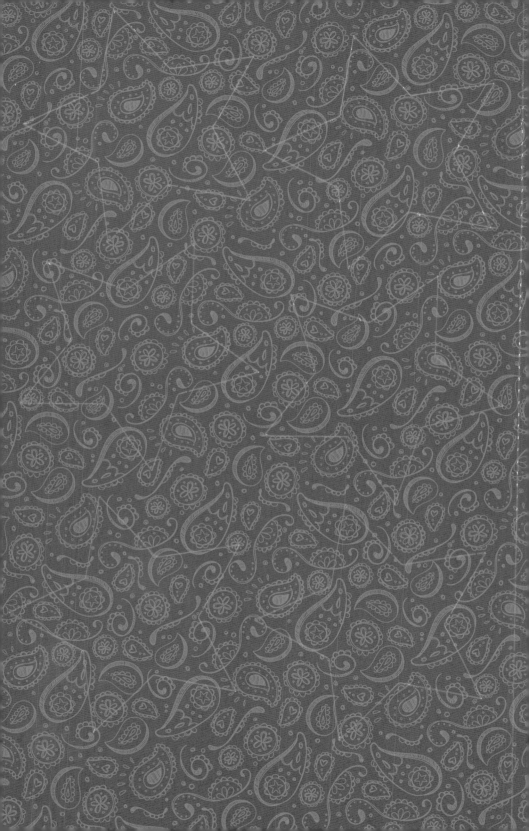